The New Human
Agreement

The New Human Agreement

✦

The 5000 Year Plan

Joshua E. Basileia

iUniverse, Inc.
New York Lincoln Shanghai

The New Human Agreement
The 5000 Year Plan

iUniverse, Inc.

For information address:
iUniverse, Inc.
2021 Pine Lake Road, Suite 100
Lincoln, NE 68512
www.iuniverse.com

ISBN: 0-595-30174-6

Printed in the United States of America

Contents

Introduction

If you are reading these words, then you are a human being living on planet Earth. That is who these words are intended for, human beings, living on planet Earth. Humans have inhabited this small planet for a very long time. Many civilizations have risen and fallen. Some have been documented, while others have not. A pattern has emerged over these many eons of time. Humans have been unable, so far, to develop a permanent and pervasive global social structure that provides *peaceful* co-existence between different cultures with different ideologies. People are barely able to co-exist with other people that have similar ideologies. There have been individual and collective successes. However, the conflicts and violence that exist today on earth clearly demonstrate that the animalistic nature of humans, with its' violent tendencies, dominates the social fabric of our small planet. Although our population now exceeds six billion, the majority of the population on earth, rarely behave in a violent manner. Most people seek and desire an ordinary peaceful existence. The fact remains that a relatively small percentage of individuals seem to have entrapped all peoples of the Earth in this unfortunate cycle of violence.

There are nine topics for discussion, and please do discuss them; with your friends, neighbors, co-workers, at your churches, mosques, synagogues, temples, and other public meeting places. These are very important topics indeed. It's not an overstatement to say that the future of all mankind hangs in the balance. These topics are designed to expose the attitudes and social morays that perpetrate negative and violent behavior patterns while preventing human progress. The ninth topic consists of a list of basic agreements that hopefully will be acceptable to most people regardless of their social or religious ideologies.

The 5000 year aspect of this work is designed to give perspective. How will human beings 5000 years from now judge our generations? How will the intellectual and emotional profile of human beings change during this time? If you look back 100 years in history, Earth was a completely different place as far as the global society is concerned. What we now consider to be appalling attitudes of the past were unquestioned by former cultures. What are the current appalling attitudes we accept and practice that we are also unaware of? Our 5000 year future will yield equally surprising results. Some of the changes to human behavior that need to be made are blindingly obvious. See if you agree.

Topic One
Geochauvinism

◆

Everyone Is From Somewhere…Else

Everyone is from somewhere…else. Think about where you live. You live in a city, town, or village. You may live in a state, a prefecture, a county, a parish, a region, a country, or perhaps a kingdom. In the area you live, you eat certain kinds of food, you wear certain types of clothes, you observe certain customs, you also expect a certain kind of weather, and you speak specific versions of language. People who do not live in your area or region are called foreigners.

At this time, there are more than six billion people living on planet earth. Even if you live in a large city with five to ten million people or more, that means that over five and a half billion people live somewhere else. This is a very important concept, because people have always considered other people who do not live in <u>their</u> area of the world to be strange and untrustworthy. Foreigners look different, talk differently, observe different customs, and hold different beliefs. The idea that everyone else is a foreigner and untrustworthy, is at the heart of human beings inability to arrive at a state of peaceful coexistence between dissimilar cultures. This concept is so fundamental, that it is often completely overlooked.

People who live in one area of the world are convinced that people who live in other areas of the world are strange and are to be disliked and distrusted due this strangeness. Even when different cultures share borders and social characteristics, the minor differences are used as the rationale for prejudice and hatred. This same attitude is also applied on the local level by people disliking and distrusting those that live "on the other side of town". Part of this notion is related to men's need to compete and to have identifiable enemies with which to set themselves against. Most people have heard the term xenophobia which pertains to the fear of outsiders or strangers. The term xenophobia is not comprehensive enough to explain modern attitudes. "Geochavinism", a new term, was designed to establish this concept. In its' most brief definition it means, to be chauvinistic about where you are from, in other words, cultural chauvinism in all its' many forms. Let's take a short ride to a place where you are the foreigner. If you were to travel a few hundred kilometers in any one direction, the culture would begin to change. The customs, the food, the drink, and the language would begin to change. You would become the foreigner. The farther you travel, the more foreign you become.

With this observation explained, how do human beings reconcile the differences between them and live in peace as neighbors without inflicting violence and death on each other over disputes involving ideology and property? Each group of people, from the many different areas of the world, all have attributes that they are proud of. These attributes are the very definition of why others see them as foreigners. What you end up with is a list of sociological attributes that create pride within the group that is described. This same list of attributes is used by others to justify bias, prejudice and hatred. Please keep in mind that everyone is from somewhere else, just like you. Geochavinism, our new word, has two meanings. The first meaning has been discussed in detail. That is, the attitude of superiority based on ones location, plus, a negative bias towards people who are not from the same area or region that you are from. This simply means to be chauvinistic about where you are from. What is the correct version of a human being and where does he or she live.

The second meaning of Geochauvinism relates more to how most people see themselves in the universe. If you go back in history, you will see that humans have struggled with several facts. They first fact is that we are living on a rotating planet, second, that this same planet travels around our sun, third, that the sun travels in its' own orbit around the center of our galaxy, and fourth, that the galaxy itself is traveling through space at incredible speeds. Few people actually relate to the universe beyond just walking around and living on the surface of a planet and even fewer relate to the motion of that planet through galactic and universal space. Universal space is just another name for the universe. There is just one large space for all matter. Most humans do not know that all the stars they see with their eyes are in our galaxy, the Milky Way, with the exception of a few smudges of light that turn out to actually be other galaxies, which are bundles of billions of stars like our galaxy. When humans are told by scientist that the Hubble telescope can peer ten to fifteen billion light years into universal space and that the borders are as yet uncertain, they find it unbelievable, hypothetical, or both. How do these ideas relate to the concept of "geochauvinism", or the second definition of this term? The second definition reveals that people think that the Earth is over here and the rest of the universe is over there, when it is really all one very big place.

It was not until people gave up the idea that the earth was flat, that they actually began to contemplate what was 'out there' as a scientific concept. Over millennia of time, different cultures arrived at more and more complex conclusions about what is 'out there'. Most of what humans knew prior to that was more about the mythology of the stars, not the reality. There have been great gains in knowledge in this area of science during the last one hundred years, with a handful of scientist completely changing human being's view of themselves by leaps of insight into atomic and cosmological truth.

In modern times, the question about whether or not there is life in "outer space", (universal space), has intrigued a great number of human beings. All across the planet there have been discussions and debates on this topic. There are many theories about the possibility although no one actually knows. Some theories are based on mathematics; others are exobiological, while some are religious or spiritual. No one has yet to answer this question. The concept of geochavinism has remained in effect. We are still waiting for a definitive answer to this question. During this time of waiting, humans have adopted an Earth centered view of the universe. Galileo spent the final years of his life imprisoned for his failure to accept the geochavinistic views of his Church. He asserted that the Earth was not the center of the universe. He was only officially exonerated at the end of the twentieth century. Incredibly, this many years later, we still hold a similar view. We accept that the Earth goes around the sun, along with the other planets, but we still see ourselves as over "here" and the rest of the universe as over "there". This seems to be based solely on the distance between stars and our current inability to "see" things clearly that are light years away. The concept of light years confuses many people so let's just say 5.8 trillion miles so that everyone reading this can grasp the reason we have such a hard time "seeing" objects in space. We ask questions about life being "out there".

I have some startling news for you, proof of life, 'out there', exist now. They are called human beings and all of the life forms present on earth. We are the life 'out there' that we have been looking for. This is not meant to be simplistic or humorous. We have to separate ourselves from the universe in order to see ourselves not in it.

Part of our current geochavinism involves the concept that planets are unique to our solar system. Only after empirical evidence was presented did this incorrect view begin to erode. Planets are a characteristic of many types of stars.

The next geochauvinistic attitude is contained in the fact that even after we accept that planets are moving around other stars routinely, we assume they are lifeless. Planet Earth and all of the life forms present demonstrate a clear example of abundant life in universal space. Humans are not over 'here' and the universe over 'there'.

We are just one galaxy in billions of galaxies. Some are larger than ours while others are smaller. Some are older and some are younger. The point is not whether humans have discovered other forms of intelligent or unintelligent life in other parts of the universe. The point is that it is geochauvinistic of humans to see themselves' as alone in the universe.

Please consider how irrational it was for men to know that the world was flat. It is equally irrational to decide that you know that there is no life in other parts of the universe.

So, the two meanings of geochauvanism are closely related. One of them refers to individuals seeing themselves over here and others, (particularly foreigners), as over there. The second meaning is on a larger scale, where we see the entire planet earth as being over here with the rest of the universe as being over there. Although geochauvanism is a new term, this ancient attitude has certainly outlived its' usefulness.

Our next topic will help explain how people are able to maintain these attitudes.

Topic Two
Group Mentality with
Rapid Generalization

◆

GMRG

This concept will come up many times because it is related to so many different areas of human behavior. This condition and its' effects, must not be over looked. Those of you familiar with logic are aware of the logical fallacy called rapid generalization. One cannot rapidly draw conclusions from sketchy generalized evidence. The reason this is called a fallacy or a falsehood is that rapid conclusions based on generalized pieces of evidence are not reliable indicators of truth. Another version of rapid generalization is that just because a lot of people accept certain facts and hold a specific belief does not prove that the underlying premises are true. Group mentality is equally straight forward. This behavior is seen in the animal kingdom in flocks of birds and herds of livestock. If you are in a crowd and someone shouts, "run", you run. There may be no evidence to indicate that it is time to run, but everyone around you is responding by running. So, you rapidly generalize that running may be the right thing to do without any direct evidence to know if running is the correct action to take. When these two characteristics are combined, rapid generalization and group mentality, they produce very powerful results, either creating help or causing harm. These two behavioral characteristics are essential ingredients in election campaigns, television news, advertising, the creating of social morays and all forms of media. These two behaviors are also involved in most of your daily lives. Examples include the clothes you select, the radio station you listen to, the conversations you have while at work or at home, the activities you participate in after work, the religion you practice and even the hair style you have selected. The negative effect of group mentality with rapid generalization is very dangerous and has resulted in massive amounts of pain and suffering including the gruesome slaughter of millions of people. The positive side of GMRG is best observed after most natural disasters have occurred. Groups of strangers, organize, administrate, and provide help to injured and hurting people. They see what has happened, and begin to behave in a manner that contributes to the healing of harm, be it by fire, flood, earthquake, tornado, hurricane, volcano, terror, or war. The negative effects of GMRG can further be seen in mob behavior. People who would ordinarily never consider violent behavior will suddenly begin to destroy property and attack strangers. This is an irrational and emotionally ignorant behavior indeed. This is also an excellent example of GMRG and it happens all over the world every day.

GMRG is the main fuel of our modern geochavinistic fires. Stated another way, the many negative attitudes that allow us to accept harm to people we don't like, is tied to generations of unquestioned social morays that are just plain wrong and harmful. However, this concept pervades so many areas of life that it remains transparent. Why do business people wear shirts with button down collars and a tie? Which cultures wear the "right" clothing and which cultures wear the "wrong" clothing? Every culture thinks they wear "normal" clothes. Who dictated the dress code in any and all cultures? Since the expression of fashion varies so greatly among cultures, what is the mechanism of dictation? The answer is GMRG–Group Mentality with Rapid Generalization. The acceptance of attitudes today because they were accepted yesterday creates the momentum for acceptance tomorrow. When you add time to this equation, the origins of these behaviors become so obscure that they are forgotten. Fashion is one simple example in a complex social web of attitudes. Are we "cattlesheep" or are we sentient? Most cultures do not appreciate individuals who question the validity of locally accepted attitudes and practices. For those rare individuals who question social, religious, and political conventions there can be great risk. And, depending on where you live, you could be beaten, imprisoned, exiled or killed, putting your whole family at risk as well. The cause of your death or imprisonment would be violent ignorance, the ignorance of those who disagree with you. The male tendency to be right and in charge contributes to so much suffering. The human animal is so ready to kill for so many reasons that the stimulus for these actions becomes extremely irrelevant.

At this point in our discussion, I would like to introduce another concept called the "spectrum of mentality". Why are some people prone to violence while others would die themselves before they would kill another person? This spectrum includes all human beings. It extends from the remaining hunter/gatherer cultures to those humans who have gazed at Earth from space through the portals of human designed space craft. In general terms, our education varies from basic to intermediate to advanced. There are also many college graduates in this group. Education and intellect have nothing to do with it. This concept does not intend to set up any notions of one group being better than another. It is the mentality of harm. Under what conditions will a person perpetrate violence or harmful actions against other people? On one end of the spectrum you have an individual that even in the midst of an angry violent mob will not consider raising their hand to harm another person. On the other end of the spectrum you have those who plan murder on a daily basis and whose highest goal is martyrdom. One might think that religious people would represent the largest peaceful and non-violent cross section of people. Unfortunately, now and in the past, religious people actually use their belief systems as the basis for violence, hatred, and bigotry. Certain social concepts are in the same category. Communism, Nazism, Marxism, all represent non-religious institutions that willing harm humans in the name of their particular social ideology. Another category is socio-religious or religious/dictatorships. Once again, the willingness to strike, imprison, and kill any and all who disagree with institutional ideology reveals the true nature of these societies, male egoism. This is the real driving force behind every single one of these. Clearly being right and in charge is a male feature of epic proportion. This concept unifies all of the above groups. It is an individual leader or a group of leaders that force and impose their views of reality on all those people under their rule or authority. The time has arrived to shine a very bright light on this dark corner of human behavior. The people who live without desiring harm to others deserve a planet where they are safe. Those same people, who are able to accept deferring views and attitudes without thoughts of control and violence, represent the people of the 5000 year plan. How will humans behave thousands of years from now when they have shed their animalistic appendages of violence? Let's begin to use the positive side of GMRG, Group Mentality with Rapid Generalization, to begin a worldwide movement in which all can participate. Let's use non-violent methods to help free the violently oppressed. We must end the period of history in which a small percentage of individuals are able to entrap an entire planet in an endless cycle of violence. This accepted behavior is detrimental to the majority of the people on earth and benefits only this small percentage of violent individuals.

Topic Three
That's Between You and the Universe

What is? Everything! Everything you are is between you and the universe; your attitudes, your beliefs, your customs, your habits, your flaws, and even your good qualities. Everything you are is between you and the universe. What is meant by this statement?

There is a judgmental aspect to human beings that is universal. It is not just religious people that are judgmental. Atheists are judgmental. Agnostics are judgmental. People from all walks of life and from all areas of the world judge other people based on external references and preconceived notions.

If your belief system is as you say it is, then, that's between you and the universe. I do not have to accept your view and you don't have to accept mine. If you believe in a judgmental God who judges all humans at the end of this age, then you have realized that you cannot stand up for or answer for any other person at the judgment. You cannot argue on their behalf, make explanations, nor change their standing with God. You can answer to no one for the actions or attitudes of other people. You stand alone when answering for yourself. We know as conscious entities that we are in a world with other people and that we are connected to all of them. We know that we are uniquely individual and ultimately responsible for our own actions, our own words, and our own thoughts.

If, in your universe, God exist, then that is between you and God. If, in your universe, God does not exist, then your life and everything contained there in, is between you and the blank stare of the universe. This does not mean that while living on Earth you are not accountable to other people for harmful or violent actions.

I would hope that one day no one will harbor hatred or prejudice toward anyone and that at some point in time people cease to harm other people. The thought is the seed, the word is the sapling, and the deed is the full grown tree. Sow seeds of peace by not judging other people based on external references. Everyone must ultimately answer for themselves. If you think that their religion is incorrect and that yours is correct, can you answer for them? No, you cannot. It is your duty to pray for them, not to hate or judge them. If you are an atheist who could care less about anyone but yourself, you still answer for your own actions, even if it is to nothing but the dirt of your grave. No one can answer to the void of space on your behalf.

Suspend judgment. Let others answer for themselves, as to how they look, what they believe, how they dress and the attitudes they have adopted. What would you do if the world was at peace? What would the next five thousand years look like if violence subsided? We have to start somewhere. We can only solve problems one at a time. The first problem we must solve is the incredibly violent nature and animalistic tendencies of human beings. These tendencies are learned behavior, not innate. The intellectual equivalent of violence is judgmentalism. It provides rational paths to hatred and prejudice. Remove these paths and take a new look at where humans are going. Stop war first. Stop fist fights later. Stop angry shouting after that. How will people behave when Earth is a peaceful place? What will an average person's emotional and social profile become after five thousand years of peace? What a bizarre world humans have created. The universe is watching us at a great distance, waiting…waiting. What will humans become as a specie? Plan for five thousand years of peace and see what you become. The universe is waiting. It has all the time in the world, literally.

Topic Four
Who Knows?

◆

Belief Systems and Science

Who knows? This topic creates the greatest amount of controversy and extracts the greatest level of emotion from human beings. The reasons for this will be clearer after we discuss some of the particulars. The foundation of a belief system is a belief. The foundations of belief systems are beliefs. If you take a belief and multiply it by seven trillion, you still have a belief. This is not meant to discourage anyone from holding beliefs. You should examine your heart and mind in regard to what you believe and why you believe it. One should never require others to adopt a particular belief system as a condition of social acceptance.

The greatest and most profound truth regarding belief systems is what all religions have in common. I do not mean by this how similar they are; in many cases they are quite dissimilar. The common foundation they all share is that…no individual or group actually knows. No one knows the answers with absolute certainty (How did the universe begin? Where did human beings come from? Which religion is correct? What happens after we die?). No matter how much rhetoric or how many volumes of exegesis exist regarding any one belief system, nobody knows. Religion is not called a knowledge system. Science suffers from the same problem. Many scientific assertions are not known. How did the universe begin? If you take any group of people, you will get a variety of answers. Regardless of the level of controversy, neither cosmologist nor clergy know the answer with absolute certainty. Scientist are still asking questions and increasing the amount of new data concerning how the universe actually began. Within most religious circles, questions are not allowed and new information is of no interest. Never the less, the most brilliant scientist and the most fundamental clergy share a profound and equalizing foundation. Neither one of them know with absolute certainty. Some think this, others believe that. Who knows? No one! Saying that you are certain about the human soul and the afterlife is absolutely unprovable in any logical sense. Saying that you are certain about what you believe is a far cry from actually knowing. How ridiculous it is to see humans argue over what is not known. Charles Darwin and the Pope have this distinction in common, however, Darwin never imprisoned anyone for disagreeing with his beliefs. These two groups look in different directions for the answer. I do not dishonor any culture's belief system or question the validity thereof. How could I. I also do not know. In science, with each new fact comes an avalanche of new questions. Discovery is at the heart of the excitement of science. Unquestioning faith is at the heart of belief systems. That is the very nature of faith, believing but not knowing.

With this simple truth in mind, how can humans argue, fight, and kill each other over facts that are not in evidence. As was stated at the beginning, humans have inhabited the earth for a very, very, long time. How long? No one knows. If you believe that it has been fifteen thousand years, you don't know. If you believe that it has been four hundred million years, you also, do not know. The answer to which version is correct pales in comparison to the horror of how people will treat each other over the unknown answer. No human or group of humans will ever be able to dogmatically defend any position on this topic again in light of this simple wisdom. No one knows.

This concept is a liberating one. It frees me to allow you to believe whatever your heart tells you to believe, not to replace your belief with my belief. Screaming and shouting about beliefs, do not increase their truth. Screaming and shouting about scientific theories do not increase the amount of data. The purposes of belief systems vary with each individual participant. Does the human who says there is no God, know? No they don't. Does the religious zealot who will kill in the name of God know? No they don't. Does the agnostic know that God is uncertain? Of course not. Should any person be shunned or harmed for failing to agree with you? If you answer yes to this question, it shows where you are in the "mentality spectrum". This type of attitude appears unbecoming of a deep and abiding faith. How can you shun any person over what you yourself do not know. The point here is not to question your faith. Your faith is between you and the universe.

This foundation contains one of the keys to unlocking permanent global peace. How can any person justify hatred and violence toward any other person when our commonality is that not one of us actually knows for sure what the answers to life's most profound and puzzling questions are? As humans have discovered regarding knowledge, there is no number that cannot be halved and there is no number that cannot be doubled. When we finally uncovered the molecule, we found the atom. When we uncovered the atom we discovered sub-atomic particles. After unraveling the sub-atomic particle, we found a ghost like probability amplitude of unknown description. After discovering a solar system, we found a galaxy. After galaxies, we discovered galactic clusters. We are now unraveling the edge of time and space where known laws do not apply. What scientific laws were present in the "singularity" prior to the big bang when there were no scientific laws and there was no "time and space" at all? Knowledge does not produce certainty, philosophically speaking.

It would serve no purpose, at this time, to descend into the quagmire of dogma, religious or scientific. In this dogma lies our original premise. A belief multiplied by any number, equals a belief. How can I hate you over what you believe when I am unable to prove what I believe? May this truth serve as a beacon around which people rally for world peace. As of today, belief systems can only be used as tools of violence by the self proclaimed ignorant, who actually worship self interest, not God. If history has taught us anything, it is that the changing of social morays is the most difficult task of all.

Topic Five
The Arbitration of
Death & Harm

✦

(The relative value of life)

This will seem difficult for some and not so difficult for others. What do I mean by this? God is no respecter of persons. The rain falls on everybody, both the good people and the bad. However, human beings are respecters of persons. Not only do we value wealthy, intelligent, and popular people, but we devalue poor, illiterate, and unpopular people. There are so many examples that it is difficult to know where to begin. So, let's start with a few questions for clarity. Which is worse, for a two year old child to die of natural causes, or a 54 year old adult to die as the result of violence? Is it worse for a 27 year old female to die of a disease, or an 18 year old male to die in an automobile accident? Is it worse for someone who is popular in the media to die, or a poor unknown wise man to die? What if five hundred people were killed in one place at one time due to the acts of violent men? Would that be worse than if five hundred people died of five hundred separate causes in five hundred different places on the same day? The examples are endless. Let's ask this another way. Which life is more valuable than any other life? The answer, each life is of equal value. Each life is of immeasurable value. The day that all people value all other people equally, many of the social problems that exist today will dissipate. The ability to assign relative value to groups, individuals, and other types of people creates a barrier. This barrier includes the concept of geochavinism or "those people over there", who already dress oddly, eat strange food, and speak a peculiar language. (Remember, all the languages you don't speak are peculiar, right?) It becomes an insurmountable social moray when humans accept hundreds of thousands, even millions of preventable deaths every year. If all of the man made causes of death and suffering were removed from Earth, there would still be tragic deaths. Nature will always have its' devastating surprises and the heavy toll of lives that goes with it. But, that does not excuse humans. We must begin to take the necessary actions to solve the suffering caused by neglect and violence. People, individuals, must stop causing death to other people on purpose.

Is it worse to die at the hands of a drunk driver or a sober driver, a young driver or an old driver? To the person who has lost a loved one, the tragedies are equal. Somehow, society is able to assign relative value to harm and is placated on an emotional level by the type of blame that can be extricated from a tragedy. One of the most bizarre aspects of life on Earth is the acceptance of the fact that a certain number of people will die or be maimed in an effort to travel from point "A" to point "B". This is accepted on a blind sacrificial level as though there is nothing that could be done about it. People hold onto a kind of irrational hope. "I hope I'm not maimed or killed in an automobile accident on the way to or from work today". If you take this same person out of their automobile, harm or kill them in many other ways, it would be considered a crime. The ability to label a tragic automobile fatality as an "accident" anesthetizes society and shows an ignorance of epic proportions. The statistics reveal a visceral abandon of the facts. If one were to suggest that until moving vehicles and other modes of transportation are made safe, (to the extent that death or maiming does not occur), no one will be allowed to drive or fly. People would not accept this. Ironically, they will get in an automobile to drive to the funeral of a friend or loved one who was killed while driving. This is an excellent example of GMRG, or group mentality with rapid generalization. Humans will not even consider giving up a mass proliferated convenience regardless of the harm. (This includes French fries). Just for the record, a highway fatality is unquestionably a violent death, a preventable violent death. The evidence of people's ability to become accustomed to types of death and harm is truly a telling tale. The versions of tragic death that people accept stand in stark contrast to the monuments that are built to other types of death.

Imagine a great stone monument standing in the middle of a public square or park. Inscribed on that monument are these words; "This monument stands in honor of, Anya Lee, a fourteen year old youth. She was not particularly well known. She made no great contributions to society. She was not known by a large number of people. She did not travel much outside of the neighborhood in which she lived and died. She died as the result of complications from pneumonia. We honor her life with this monument because we consider her life to be equally valuable to the lives of all other human beings on earth".

I am not aware that such a monument exists. Our inability to honor ordinary people says way more about us than our ability to honor great individuals. Each life is sacred. Each life is of equal value to God, who is not a respecter of persons.

The arbitration of death and harm is a human characteristic. It is time to change the minds of those people who have adopted elitist and class oriented attitudes. No person is better than any other person. We are all created equal. What a concept!

We must begin today to seek out all areas of the planet where people are harmed and killed, where life is not honored. Do these deaths mean nothing? Why should you care about people you don't know who live in a part of the world where you have never been? I'm sure you have figured it out by now. Everyone is from somewhere else.

Topic Six
Reverse Eden

What does this mean? In the story of Adam and Eve, instead of the female offering the male a bite of the fruit, which caused the female to be blamed for the fall of humankind throughout history, hasn't the male always dictated which fruit was to be eaten, how much, and when. Although in modern times most people agree that there was equal culpability in the story of Eden, men's hearts often run contrary to their rhetoric.

Men have ruled, regulated, and claimed superiority over women. They have started empires, countries, and companies. They have made up and dispensed laws, regulated social morays, imposed belief systems and have ruled the planet as far back as written history reveals. More importantly, men have killed other humans with impunity throughout this same shameful history. The resounding evidence shows that men, hold the personal responsibility for the failure to bring about a workable global social structure.

Women have an indirect responsibility for the lack of a workable global social structure. Their failure is stated simply. Men have dictated which fruit will be eaten and women have eaten it ever since. This is the meaning of reverse Eden. The answer to how this occurs is equally simple—violence. Due to his physical strength, men have subdued women throughout history. The key to beginning this permanent global change began only in the last century when women were given the right to vote. Physical strength and weaponry were replaced forever with the concept of, one person, one vote. This idea obviously only pertains to societies where women are "allowed" to vote. Who is "disallowing" women to do anything? Men. I'll give you a clear example of this "allow/disallow" attitude that reveals the preposterous contortions men require of women. And believe me, there are volumes of examples. In certain strict Muslim societies, women must wear "burka" to go out into public. If the foundation for this social moray is lust, why don't men wear blindfolds or a burka when they are in public? This would accomplish the same social objective. This attitude profoundly blames women for being physically appealing and places the burden of men's attitudes on the backs of women. This is so irrational that the only explanation is that violence created this behavior in women. To this day women who live in this type of socio-cultural setting are physically beaten with sticks and raped for failing to comply. And the women, again, are blamed for the beating and the rape. This sickens me to depths of my soul as do many other examples of group mentality with rapid generalization. Only a coward would enforce such a ridiculous social moray. As a footnote to this single example, the men who hold this belief would gladly kill me for exposing this awful evil. I do not mean to single out Muslims as a group because the above example pertains only to the individuals who behave in such a fashion. All religions and societies have their own version of male induced contortions on the female gender. That's what men do. They kill or injure any person who interferes with their ability to be right and in charge. Unfortunately for women, even after gaining the right to vote, men have drawn them into the testosterone laden political landscape where there are only two teams, liberals and conservatives, democrats and republicans, etc. etc. What a grand mal farce. Men's competitive nature has created a system that separates women along the same ideological lines with a large group of women voting however their husbands vote. This creates an atmosphere that makes winning the contest more important than making needed changes. It also allows men to hold onto power and continue dictating which fruit will be eaten. To add insult to injury, good men have been unable to stop the brutalization and objectification of the female gender even in the most civilized societies.

For now, let's look at the modern workplace as a prime example. Men have subjugated women and other men on a massive scale. Inequity abounds. Men create a rigid structure from which to dictate. Women, for the most part, have acquiesced. The 8:00 am to 5:00 pm schedule itself it a product of men who leave the raising of children and home management to women. This has caused a tremendous amount of stress on women who are in families where both partners work. There is even more stress in the case of a single mom or dad. The ability to keep a flexible schedule in order to increase the parent's participation in the lives of their children has been opposed by men up until recent times. This is still a point of contention in many countries and companies. For women, getting similar pay for similar work is still a valid issue today. How are men able to get away with this? Women let them. Remember, women only began to venture into the "conventional" workplace in the last fifty years! This, by itself, is an amazing fact. The reduction and/or elimination of sexual harassment was not addressed until the 1990's. Men do not give up power without a fight. They have emotional issues.(See the next topic).

Reverse Eden is not feminism. It is simply an attempt to balance a world that is overrun by men who cause a great deal of violence in the name of being right and in charge. Look at the ratio of men to women in prison populations. Women who understand the meaning of Reverse Eden can change the world for the better forever. The rest will be history.

Topic Seven
Emotional Intelligence

✦

The Lizard Must Die

The human race has excelled in the gathering of facts, inventing complex machines and building immense structures. In this rush for information, the most important attribute that all men and women possess has been totally neglected—their emotions. Human's emotional quotient, or EQ, is disproportionately low compared to their intellect, or IQ. Our modern educational systems ignore the importance of teaching young children a healthy understanding of the role their emotions play in daily life. By not educating our young children about emotional intelligence, we are hindering the progress of the human race. With the former topic in mind, (Reverse Eden), women typically have a higher EQ than the average man. Men have contended that women are the "emotional" gender. Women accept this for the most part. This is a great and pervasive falsehood. Part of the problem is that women have allowed men to use the fact that women cry more often as evidence. We all know big boys don't cry. The real evidence is the actions men take due to anger. Tears heal, anger harms. This is another large example of GMRG, or group mentality with rapid generalization. The reason men and boys behave the way they behave is due to social attitudes that were accepted so long ago that they are no longer questioned.

If you were to sit in on a board meeting of a large corporation that is dominated by men or a session of the U.S. Senate, you would see rather quickly just how emotional men are. They form their response based on what their ego perceives. The ego represents the emotional self in this regard. Men embrace those who agree with them and seek to destroy those who don't. The problem is that men do not see the actions they take as being driven by emotion. The "board meeting" is a very generalized application. Male emotion is the root cause of almost all wars and conflict on the planet Earth. Women, generally speaking, do not come to blows over disagreements. Women have rarely caused or initiated war. Further evidence of men's emotional ignorance is found in prisons all over the world. Women just simply are not enamored with violence to the extent men are. This is not an attempt to exonerate women from the harm they may have caused; they just aren't the main instigators of violence on planet Earth. In the past and even today, if women don't do what men say, men get emotional and shout, hit, or worse. There is no excuse for this kind of behavior. There is a reason however—low EQ, (emotional quotient). A positive footnote is that the number of men who would not harm women in the name of being right and in charge is increasing every day. Men and women both need to raise their collective EQ's. Society in general has looked the other way in regards to how men's emotions have shaped and directed history. A suicide bomber, whether male or female, actually represents an emotional bomb waiting to go off. The result is violence with dead bodies everywhere. The response to this emotional outburst will be a reciprocal emotional outburst of greater magnitude. The person or group who sponsors this form of murder is admitting that it is alright to murder innocent people in their families as well. An old and simple version of this is stated, "If you think it is acceptable to hit people with sticks, how can you act surprised when someone hits you with the same stick?" To strike others is the same as striking self. The greatest emotional outburst ever created by humans is the nuclear bomb. It is also the greatest display of emotional ignorance. When weaponry becomes the pinnacle of group expression and conflict resolution, the largest most destructive weapon becomes the highest achievement. This is clearly shown in our modern world by the insistence of more and more undemocratic countries to acquire "WMD", weapons of mass destruction. Please let this previous statement dwell in your mind and soul; "mass destruction". The New Human Agreement can only institute "IMH", instrument of mass healing. Weapons of mass destruction can contain evil men for a limited period of history and we are nearing its' end. When the wrong person or group finally deploys a weapon of mass destruction, the original purpose for the creation of these weapons has been permanently undermined. Please refer to the corresponding poster called "Emotion Kills, Emotion Heals". It isn't idealistic to state that we must eliminate these obscene weapons. It is idealistic to imagine that "mass destruction" is not inevitable under the current social global structure.

In spite of all of the above statements these are exciting times for those of us who are interested in human progress. A large group of people have realized and envisioned a less violent world in which ordinary people can pursue happiness without the fear of violence. The lizard must die. The lizard is the cold blooded animal that remains in the souls of many humans, much like the appendix which lingers in the body as a vestige of what was once needed, but is no longer. The sword of the past is being replaced by the social morays of the future. We must educate the children of today in new ways and clarify the role of emotional intelligence, now and in the near future. In the meantime, we must try to define the emotional profile of what people will be like five thousand years from now when we will make war no more.

Topic Eight
Rotten Apples

When you consider the small percentage of individuals that are able to ruin the quest for ordinary life for most people, it represents an extraordinary statement. Of the six billion people living on planet Earth, less than a few thousand male humans direct the majority of slaughter, injustice, hunger, oppression and violence on the earth. I said <u>direct</u>, not carry out. This deplorable fact does not take into account the daily crimes of assault, theft, and senseless harm caused by others individual "crimes", some of these are on purpose and some are unintended. This fact also includes the vast armies of all nations that are under the rule of a very small number of "leaders". This statement is best exemplified by one of these armies. A handful of men dictate the actions of all the men in the army and this handful of men answer to one man. From one perspective it appears that the individual is aiming and firing the weapon. Who does the soldier shoot? Why and when does he shoot his weapon? This is rigidly dictated by leadership who ultimately answer to one man. The conditions that cause individuals to carry out violence against other people at the instruction of leaders vary widely. Societies are the same way. There may be less structure to the chain of command, like a street gang, but the individuals still rigidly obey, even when they are not conscience of their obedience. The focus here is on the megalomaniacal despots who have taken the concept of violence, in the name of ideology, property, and power, to inhumane heights. These individuals literally own and dictate everything that happens in whole countries. This ownership includes the people in these countries. It is bad enough when they own whole companies and ruin the lives of individuals. Either way, the whole barrel is ruined and the barrel is full of sacred and immeasurably valuable souls. The term communism or Marxism is most perverse and convoluted when used to justify and explain the acts of these individuals. No social or cultural term will serve to cover up the atrocities that are actually going on in these countries. <u>Violentism</u> is the only acceptable term and you won't hear that term used on any news broadcast. If an individual within one of these countries disagrees openly with the leadership or the government, they are physically beaten, imprisoned, exiled, or killed. Under these condi-tions there is no communism or Marxism; there is only unilateral negotiation under duress. No one can be expected to honor the terms imposed under these conditions. The leaders of these countries know the truth. Their people would flee or overthrow them in a second if they had the chance or the ability. These megalomaniac's egos have become so large that their souls have completely fled. Mass political murder and imprisonment in the name of being right and in charge is a male feature of epic proportion. The terrible effect of this human ani-mal characteristic cannot be measured since each human life is of immeasurable value.

The point of this section is that under the terms outlined in the new human agreement, these pockets of violence and despotism will gradu-ally fade until there are no more left. Certain societies won't be forced to worship these tyrants as many are forced to today; not because they want to, but because they are forced to. Many of the people who find themselves' living in these oppressive social environments seem to pos-sess an instinctive survival reaction. This overpowering instinct of sur-vival exposes the eternal spirit within each of us acknowledging the sacredness of life.

If you look at the entire planet as of today, even with all the violent conflict, most of the Earth and most of the people on it are not directly involved in violent behavior. The negative effect of a few bad apples pervades the ordinary lives of most peaceful people. Peaceful people are the majority. Women and children are the majority. To add obscene insult to perverse injury, peaceful people, women and children who are killed unintentionally during times of war are classified as "collateral damage".

The barrel of life is full of sacred souls. The rotten apples need to get their own planet. In the mean time perhaps we can give the rotten apples an island where they can murder each other with impunity and leave the greater majority of peaceful humans in peace. When there is no one left on the island, the whole Earth will be at peace. What will the Earth be like after five thousand years of peace?

Topic Nine
Can We Agree?

As you may have noticed, this work is entitled "The New Human Agreement". It appears that we have only discussed what is wrong with current social constructs. The eight topics that we have discussed so far are designed as foundations for agreement. These previous topics are also designed to expose the fundamental attitudes that are creating barriers to a permanent peaceful global social structure. In this final section we list the fundamental rights of all peoples. These may appear to be self evident truths, but if that were the case, why are there so many oppressed and suffering people. Let's attempt to create the shortest list that we can agree on and expand it as the peoples of the Earth strive to reduce suffering and create peace. In the second book of the New Human Agreement series, we will elaborate more on the nuts and bolts of accomplishing a permanent peaceful global social structure and we will confront more directly the identifiable people who cause the greatest amount of preventable suffering. First, we must tackle some of the social morays that are preventing progress.

Can we agree on these things?

1) All humans deserve: 1) food, 2) clothing, 3) shelter, 4) clean water, 5) access to medical treatment, 6) access to information and an education, 7) protection from violence.
Which one of these do you disagree with and why? Should any individual or group be allowed to withhold any one of these things from any other person and under what conditions?

2) Can we agree that most people are not violent and seek an ordinary peaceful existence?

3) Can we agree that no person should be forced under threat of violence to adopt any particular attitude, belief system, social system, or political philosophy?

4) Can we agree that all people are endowed with certain inalienable rights and that these rights include; freedom of expression, freedom of religion, freedom of the press, and freedom from unreasonable search and seizure, freedom from violence, freedom to own personal property, and the freedom to pursue happiness?

5) Can we agree that all people are created equal?

6) Can we agree that only people who seek to impose their own personal views of reality on others would disagree with the first five agreements?

7) Can we agree that a permanent peaceful global social structure is a goal worth achieving and is in the best interest of all people?

8) Can we agree that the proliferation of violent conflict and actions must come to an end?

9) Can we agree that condoning violence against others automatically condones violence against self?

10) Can we agree that if enough people agree, we can change the world?

In closing, there is no "one world". There is however, at this time, only one planet. What will you and the future generations of the human race become in five thousand years? A journey of five thousand years begins with a single moment.

About the Author

As a young child, Joshua E. Basileia lived in many different U.S. cities and Germany. He noticed a pattern in human behavior that intrigued him even at an early age. As an adult, he sensed an overwhelming duty to expose the social morays that continue to cause harm while preventing the progress of a permanent peaceful global social structure. Joshua E. Basileia currently lives with his wife and two children in Alabama.

0-595-30174-6